W9-AAE-424

THE
ULTIMATE
invisible ink
ACTIVITY BOOK

super-secret
THE ^OWNER OF THIS BOOK IS,

- ,

ALSO KNOWN BY CODE NAME

- .

⚡ WARNING ⚡

KLUTZ® creates activity books and other great stuff for kids ages 3 to 103. We began our corporate life in 1977 in a garage we shared with a Chevrolet Impala. Although we've outgrown that first office, Klutz galactic headquarters is still staffed entirely by real human beings. For those of you who collect mission statements, here's ours:

CREATE WONDERFUL THINGS • BE GOOD • HAVE FUN

Book printed in Jiaxing City, China. 68
UV Pen made in Guangzhou, China. 99

WRITE US
We would love to hear your comments regarding this or any of our books.

KLUTZ®
557 Broadway
New York, NY 10012
thefolks@klutz.com

Distributed in Australia by
Scholastic Australia Ltd
PO Box 579
Gosford, NSW
Australia 2250

Distributed in Hong Kong by
Scholastic Hong Kong Ltd
Suites 2001-2, Top Glory Tower
262 Gloucester Road
Causeway Bay, Hong Kong

ISBN 978-1-338-74528-3
4 1 5 8 5 7 0 8

FSC
www.fsc.org
MIX
Paper from
responsible sources
FSC® C135401

We make Klutz books using resources that have been approved according to the FSC® standard which is managed by the Forest Stewardship Council®. This means the paper in this book comes from well-managed FSC®-certified forests and other controlled sources.

Stock photos ©Shutterstock.com

THE NOT-SO-SECRET LIST OF FUN STUFF YOU'LL FIND INSIDE

BORED? NOT ANYMORE!

Lucky you! You are the proud owner of a brand-new, super-secret, really cool UV pen! This pen has many highly important powers, so be sure to use it wisely.

1 UV LIGHT   **2 UV LIGHT SWITCH**

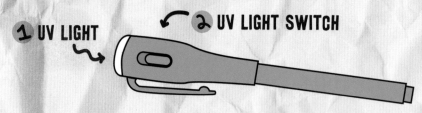

THINGS YOUR PEN CAN DO:

✓ Write in invisible ink. (Try it!)

✓ Reveal the invisible ink with the special UV light. (But don't look into it!)

✓ Help spot hidden images and printing in this very book.

✓ Give you HOURS of fun stuff to do!

THINGS YOUR PEN CANNOT DO:

✗ Help you get out of cleaning your room.

✗ Turn a bad hair day into a good hair day.

✗ Convince your parents to buy you a pony.

✗ Conduct magic spells (but it would look pretty cool as a wand).

TRY IT! Try writing your name to the right with your new pen. If this is your first time using the pen, you will need to remove the plastic tab at the top. You don't see anything, right? Now push the button on the cap and shine the light on the box. Can you see it now? Amazing, right?! (And always remember, never look directly at the light or shine it in anyone's eyes!)

PRO TIP Always put the cap on your pen when you're done using it! If the tip of the pen seems dry, dip it in some water to help. Never color over marker, crayon, pencil, or paint! This will ruin or discolor your marker cap. (BOO!)

WHAT IN THE WORLD IS UV LIGHT?

Ultraviolet light, UV light for short, is part of the light spectrum that human eyes can't see. We only see red, orange, yellow, green, blue, indigo, and violet. You can imagine UV light hanging out at the end of the rainbow.

Infrared

Shine your UV pen light next to the rainbow. Do you see something?

5 ULTRA-FASCINATING FACTS ABOUT ULTRAVIOLET LIGHT

1. "Ultraviolet" means "beyond violet."

2. UV light can kill certain types of germs, but only in certain conditions.

3. Bees can see UV light—it helps them find pollen.

4. Scorpions glow under UV light.

5. When used with a special powder, UV light can help detect fingerprints and shoe prints.

WHAT CAN YOU DO WITH UV LIGHT?

Keep secrets, solve mysteries, play games, and more! Keep reading to find out how to put the "U" in "UV"!

PROTECT YOUR EYES!

This light is only for revealing top-secret codes and hidden messages. Never look directly into the light!

MY (SUPER-SECRET) LIFE

Some people tell everyone everything—they have no secrets to hide. Others like to keep things to themselves and share only when they feel comfortable.

Fill in the blanks below. If you're an open book, you can write everything in regular pen. If you want to keep a few secrets to yourself, use the UV pen that comes with this book.

My full name is: _____

If I could change my name, I would change it to _____

_____

_____.

I am _____ **years old.**

My birthday is: _____.

I live in: _____.

My best friends are named _____.

My friends make me feel: (circle one) 😍　　😕　　😐　　😭

The thing I love most about my friends is _____.

My favorite memory with them is _____

_____

_____

My school is named _____.

I'm in _____ **grade and my teacher is** _____.

These things make me feel ... (circle one per line)

	😍	💀	🙄	😭
Math				
Writing				
Homework				
Talking in front of the class				
Basketball				
Soccer				
Dancing				
Painting/drawing				
Keeping my room clean				
Gaming				
Reading				
Chores				
Crafting				
Candy				
Chips				
Pickles				
Wearing fancy clothes				

THERE'S A MYSTERY IN THIS BOOK

CRIME — It was a crime of sugar-covered passion. A vanilla birthday cupcake with rainbow-colored frosting disappeared from the kitchen counter.

YOUR MISSION — Catch the culprit

VICTIM — Emma, the birthday girl

TIME — Approximately 3:04 p.m.

DAY — Emma's birthday, March 21

PLACE — Emma's kitchen

PRO TIP

Make sure to use the UV pen on this page to collect all the info on each suspect!

So... whodunnit?

Emma	Ollie	Shanice
→ Birthday girl	→ Emma's younger brother	→ Emma's BFF
→ Loves dessert, rainbows, and birthdays	→ Lots of energy, easily amused	→ Perfectionist, loves to cook and bake
→ Potential motive: didn't want to share her cupcake with her brother after her birthday dinner	→ Potential motive: thought it would be fun to pull a prank on his big sis	→ Potential motive: decided the rainbow cupcake's frosting didn't meet her standards

Each clue below will lead you to a number. Flip to that page number and use your UV pen light to search for frosting-covered fingerprints. Match them up to the correct suspect and tally the number of fingerprints for each. Whoever left the most fingerprints in this book is the cupcake thief. Turn to page 59 to find the answer.

Clue #1: Some people think this number is good luck.

Clue #2: Some people think this number is bad luck.

Clue #3: If you have 10 bicycles, you have this many wheels.

Clue #4: On a leap year, February has this many days.

Clue #5: America has this many states.

Clue #6: One hour has this many minutes.

ISN'T SOLVING MYSTERIES SWEET? ;)

Struggling to find the right pages?
Flip to page 59 to find where they are!

In real life, fingerprinting isn't 100% accurate. But in this book, fingerprints will lead you right to the thief!

To Lift Fingerprints

If you suspect someone mishandled your stuff, you can try to pick up a real-life fingerprint with this technique. Make sure to clean up any cocoa powder after. (You want to get fingerprints, not bugs!)

1 Sprinkle cocoa powder where the fingerprint is.

2 Lightly use a soft paintbrush to encourage the print to appear.

3 Stick a piece of clear tape directly on the fingerprint.

4 Carefully unpeel the tape and stick it on a sheet of white paper.

THERE'S AN A-Z SCAVENGER HUNT IN THIS BOOK

Use your UV pen to search this book as you read! Shine your UV pen to see if you can find these items hidden in invisible ink throughout these pages. Once you uncover the object, check it off the list!

- ☐ Alien
- ☐ Backpack
- ☐ Crayon
- ☐ Dinosaur
- ☐ Emoji
- ☐ Flashlight
- ☐ Guitar
- ☐ Hat
- ☐ Ice cream
- ☐ Jellyfish
- ☐ Kite
- ☐ Lightning bolt
- ☐ Magnifying glass
- ☐ Narwhal
- ☐ Octopus
- ☐ Pig
- ☐ Queen
- ☐ Rainbow
- ☐ Submarine
- ☐ Tree
- ☐ Uranus
- ☐ Volcano
- ☐ Wave
- ☐ X-ray vision
- ☐ You
- ☐ Zap!

PRO TIP
Shine your light on this apple to see what each image will look like:

HAVING TROUBLE? GIVE UP?
Flip to page 58 to see where you can find these!

FINDERS KEEPERS

Want to keep the hunt going? Create a UV scavenger hunt in your own house!

1 Grab any five small items (they should be about the size of your fist) and hide them. Don't be afraid to hide them somewhere really hard to find.

2 Write the name of each item on a checklist for your "finder."

3 Draw a map of the hiding area. Then use your UV pen to make an "X" in the location of each hidden item so that it looks like a treasure map.

4 Tell the finder to use the UV pen light to find the treasure!

WHAT ARE SOME ITEMS YOU COULD HIDE?
List some ideas below! Then, use the space to practice drawing your treasure map!

_____

_____

_____

_____

_____

THERE'S A RIDDLE IN THIS BOOK

There's an ultra-secret, triple-secure riddle in this book. It's hard to find and even harder to answer.

This is a type of code that requires some careful attention to detail ... because if everyone could read it right away, it wouldn't be a secret!

Ready for the challenge?

Use your UV pen light to find three numbers under each line. Those three numbers will lead you to a word:

→ The first number tells you which page to turn to.

→ The second number tells you which line on the page to find the word. (Start counting from the top of the page!)

→ The third number tells you which word on the line to add to the riddle.

As you find each word, write it on the line below. Once you've found all of the words, use your UV pen to search this page to see if you got the riddle correct—and you can reveal the answer, too!

You throw away the _____, then _____ the inside.

Then you _____ the outside, and _____ away the inside.

What is it?

_____

CAN'T FIGURE OUT THE ANSWER? Use your pen to guide you!

MAKE YOUR OWN RIDDLE!

In an old magazine or newspaper, highlight letters to make your very own secret message.

Local Super Genius Saves the Day

50 CENTS

APRIL 13, 1987 · AFTERNOON EDITION

Taylor Johnson, a 12-year-old super genius, has saved us all. Tuesday afternoon was pleasant and sunny in Everywhereville-town. Johnson was sitting on a bench enjoying the day. "Sometimes I like to bring my dog with me and get some fresh air," Johnson said.

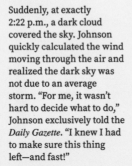

Suddenly, at exactly 2:22 p.m., a dark cloud covered the sky. Johnson quickly calculated the wind moving through the air and realized the dark sky was not due to an average storm. "For me, it wasn't hard to decide what to do," Johnson exclusively told the *Daily Gazette*. "I knew I had to make sure this thing left—and fast!"

The weather front was, in fact, being caused by an Unidentified Giant Hovercraft, also known as, an UGH. Johnson sprang into action. "I left my dog, Fillmore sitting on the bench and ran toward the UGH," Johnson recalled. "It was pretty high up, so I had to climb a tree, and then climb on to the roof of the ice cream shop. And from there the rest was easy. I made a makeshift kite out of a pizza box and my shoelace. From there, it was nothing. I just had to harness the wind and throw the 358 ton UGH out of the atmosphere."

When asked by local scientists, mathematicians, and curious citizens exactly how he was capable of such a feat, Johnson replied "Ugh, please, let's just be glad it's gone!"

Now write out some clues for the "decoder" or the person who will read the message. Your decoder will need to borrow your UV pen to figure out what you're trying to tell them.

Use this page as a practice space! Highlight some words or letters above and create a code. What does your message say?

HIDING IN PLAIN SIGHT

Some of the things you see every day have secrets you may have never even thought about. Take a guess and fill in the blanks below. Use your UV pen light to check your answers at the bottom of the page.

① Many backpacks have a _____ built into the buckle.

② Bubbles in a bathtub aren't just to help you get clean. They also help keep the water from getting _____.

③ The purpose of the little _____ at the side edges of escalators is to keep your shoelaces and other pieces of clothing (or body parts!) from getting tangled in the steps.

④ The tiny round hole at the top of the elevator door is a _____.

⑤ You know the tab that helps you open a soda can? If you flip it over, it can perfectly hold a _____.

⑥ There is only one king in a deck of cards that doesn't have a mustache. It's the king of _____. The mustache was lost due to poor printing processes through the years.

⑦ _____ were originally added to the top of sailors' hats to keep them from bumping their heads on low ceilings. Now you can find them on winter hats just for fun!

⑧ The teeny-tiny hip pocket on the outside of your jeans was originally added in the 1800s to store your _____.

HIDING IN YOUR HOME

You already have a ton of stuff that glows under UV light—including some of the things you eat!

Go on a UV expedition right at home. See how many items on the list you can find. Then use the UV pen light to see if the items glow. Add anything else you found along the way that glows, too!

ITEM	DID YOU FIND IT?	DOES IT GLOW UNDER UV LIGHT?
Building bricks		
Cotton balls		
Highlighter ink		
Anything neon		
Honey		
Ketchup		
Olive oil		
Pipe cleaners		
Tonic water		
Turmeric (a spice)		
Banana		

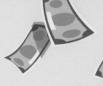

HIDING IN YOUR POCKET

Did you know there are a bunch of secret messages hidden right on the back of a dollar bill?!

Shine your UV light on the dollar bill on the next page to get a better look at some semi-hidden messages.

1 Do you see the words on the eagle's banner? This motto doesn't just appear on the dollar—it's important enough to be required on every coin! The Latin words translate to: "Out of many, one." The modern interpretation of this refers to the melting pot of America, but it originally represented the unit of the early states.

2 The letters "MDCCLXXVI" you see at the bottom of the pyramid aren't a secret code—they're the Roman numerals for 1776, the year America declared independence.

3 Wonder why the eagle is holding 13 arrows, with 13 stars, 13 stripes, and 13 olives nestled among the leaves? They all represent the 13 original colonies.

YOUR MONEY, YOUR WAY

The design of more valuable U.S. dollars, like the $20 and the $100 bill, has been changing to make them even harder for counterfeiters to copy. (Counterfeiters are people who create and use fake money.) Bills now have security ribbons, images that change color, faint designs that are only visible in certain light, and other hidden signs.

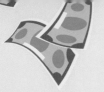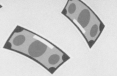

WHAT SECRET MESSAGES WOULD YOU HIDE ON A DOLLAR?

Try designing your own version of a dollar bill and include cryptic images, invisible ink, or secret codes to keep it looking snazzy—and keep it safe from counterfeiters.

front

back

DIY INVISIBLE INK

The UV pen that comes with this book is pretty cool, but the ink won't last forever. Don't worry if you run out—it's really easy to make your own invisible ink at home! Here are two ways to do it.

The Crayon Method

SUPPLIES

- ☐ White crayon
- ☐ Paintbrush
- ☐ White paper
- ☐ Watercolor paint

WRITE

1. Use the crayon to write on the white paper, just as you would normally. It's a little bit tricky because you won't be able to see what you're writing!

REVEAL

1. Wet the paintbrush and dip it in the watercolors.
2. Paint the sheet of paper lightly.
3. You'll see the secret message appear through the paint.

 HOW DO PARENTS ALWAYS KNOW WHEN THEIR INVISIBLE KIDS AREN'T TELLING THE TRUTH?

USE YOUR UV PEN TO REVEAL THE ANSWER!

The Lemon Method

SUPPLIES

- ☐ ½ lemon (have an adult help you cut it)
- ☐ ½ teaspoon water
- ☐ Bowl
- ☐ Spoon
- ☐ Cotton swab
- ☐ White paper
- ☐ Lamp with lightbulb

MAKE

1. Squeeze the lemon juice into the bowl.
2. Pour the water into a bowl and mix with a spoon.

WRITE

1. Dunk the cotton swab in the water and let it soak up the lemon-water mixture.
2. Use the wet cotton swab to write a secret message on a piece of paper.
3. Let the paper dry.

REVEAL

1. Hold the paper up to the lamp. (Be careful not to get too close!)
2. Your secret message will appear like magic!

HAHA

WHY DIDN'T THE INVISIBLE KIDS JOIN THE ALL-STAR SOCCER TEAM?

USE YOUR UV PEN TO REVEAL THE ANSWER!

PRANK BREAK!

You know what's totally NOT boring? Playing a little joke on someone. It is SO exciting waiting for them to find out what you've done because you never know what their reaction will be!

IMPORTANT

Make sure to keep your pranks light and funny—not mean. And remember...if you play a prank on someone, they just might play a prank on you!

THE ULTIMATE, FOOLPROOF,

100% GUARANTEED-TO-GET-LAUGHS,

 ## BEST PRANK OF ALL TIME

This prank is so good, so funny, and so easy to do that we had to keep it a secret . . . until now. You'll find the instructions hidden on this page in invisible ink. So grab your UV pen, start searching, and get ready to laugh!

Diary of a Hilarious Prankster

1 This prank requires a bit of acting. But to get set up, write a few fake diary entries in your diary or notebook with a regular pen. It'll be more convincing if you add real details from your life. It should look something like this:

> Monday, October 4:
>
> I had a great day at school today. Got an A on my spelling test and got the solo in the chorus concert!

2 After a few fake entries, write a final entry that looks like this:

> Diary, I have something to tell you that I've never told anyone before. I don't even know if I can write it down. It's 100% TOP SECRET. Don't tell anyone, k? I'm going to write it in invisible ink. Here it is . . .

And then with your UV pen, write:

> GOTCHA!!!! YOU'VE BEEN PRANKED!

3 Now comes the acting part. With the diary and UV pen in hand, talk about how many secrets you've written in your diary while your target is in the room.

4 Leave your diary and pen out on your bed or dresser in a way that makes it look like you just forgot to put it away.

5 Wait to see how long it takes for your target to start snooping!

CIPHERS, CODES, AND CRYPTOGRAPHY_

CRACK THE CODE!

Have you ever secretly passed someone a note in school? Used code words with a friend so other people won't know what you're talking about? Worked out a secret way to communicate with your siblings after bedtime?

You might already be a cryptographer without even knowing it!

Cryptography is the study of ways to send and receive secret messages. It's been around forever—since way back in ancient times. Over the years, secret messages have helped protect new discoveries and win wars. Today, cryptographers use methods of coding to make sure the Internet stays safe for everyone using it.

FANCY CRYPTOLOGY WORDS THAT WILL MAKE YOU SOUND LIKE AN EXPERT

→ Plaintext: the message you're trying to send without any special characters or symbols (like emojis!)

→ Ciphertext: the message after it's been scrambled into code

→ Encryption: turning plaintext into ciphertext (scrambling secret messages)

→ Decryption: turning ciphertext back into plaintext (unscrambling secret messages)

Really ^Fake IDs

Need a fake ID fast? Cut out the IDs below and add your details!

PRO TIP

Officials often test to see if badges are official by looking for certain UV images on them. Use your UV light on these tags to see what images you find!

Special Agent

ID# 354278

CLASSIFIED

_____
signature

2667314

FBI

Criminal Cyber Services Division

Assistant Special Agent-in-Charge

_____
name

Central Intelligence Agency

Agent Name: _____

Agent ID #: _____

Level 5 clearance

Expires: 07/12/2095

**This card holds cash value.
If found, place in any mailbox.**

CODE NAME GENERATOR

Super-secret spies have code names to keep their true identities a secret. Your code name can be absolutely anything you can dream up, but if you want ideas to get started try this code name generator.

For your first name, use the name of your first pet.

For your last name, find the month you were born in this chart, and then use the food listed next to that month.

So your code name might be:
- Rusty Tater Tot
- Lucky Boysenberry
- Fluffy Popsicle

BIRTH MONTH	LAST NAME
January	Hot Dog
February	Chicken Fingers
March	Spaghetti
April	Banana
May	Ice Pop
June	French Fries
July	Taco
August	Meatball
September	Tater Tot
October	Boysenberry
November	Nacho
December	Lasagna

Never had a pet? Use the name of your favorite animal from a TV show or movie!

WRITE YOUR CODE NAME IN INVISIBLE INK
Your code name is

CREATE YOUR OWN:
SPY LEGEND

A legend is a fake backstory spies use to cover up their identity. Fill in the blanks to create your own legend. For more of a laugh, you can list off the types of words to a friend and fill in their answers, and they'll do the same for you. If you want to keep your legend a secret, write in invisible ink!

I was born on a _____ day in _____ in
(TYPE OF WEATHER)   (MONTH)

_____. Everyone said I was the only _____
(CITY/TOWN)   (ADJECTIVE)

baby in the hospital. I could _____ before I could walk, so
(VERB)

everyone thought I was destined to win the gold medal at

_____.
(OLYMPIC SPORT)

My _____ was a(n) _____ and my _____ was
(GUARDIAN)   (PROFESSION)   (GUARDIAN)

a(n) _____ and my _____ siblings were always at
(PROFESSION)   (NUMBER HIGHER THAN 1)

_____, so I spent a lot of time on my own as a toddler. The
(AFTERSCHOOL ACTIVITY)

best part about it was that I had time to learn to _____.
(SKILL)

In school, I was surrounded by _____ kids. They liked to
(ADJECTIVE)

_____. I liked to _____. I sure didn't like it
(VERB)   (VERB)

when teachers told me not to _____. But I always carried
(VERB)

three things in my backpack to get me through the day. They were my:

_____, _____, and _____.

It may seem silly, but because I've always lived in _____,
(PLACE)

I've always wanted to go to _____. In my dreams, it's so
(PLACE)

_____ there. I tell everyone about it. When I get there someday,
(ADJECTIVE)

I want to _____ and _____ and never go home.
(VERB) (VERB)

That brings us to today. I am a(n) _____ student and a(n)
(ADJECTIVE)

_____ kid who is really good at _____ and
(ADJECTIVE) (SPORT)

_____. I love to eat _____, and I'm pretty good
(SKILL) (FOOD)

at making _____, too. Even though I'm _____ now,
(FOOD) (ADJECTIVE)

I really want to be a(n) _____ when I grow up, and I want to
(PROFESSION)

use my _____ to make that happen.
(SKILL)

Now, you can memorize your spy legend (no matter how
ridiculous it is!). Have a friend pretend to meet you for
the first time and ask get-to-know-you questions to see
if you can remember your backstory!

LEGEND IN YOUR POCKET

Here's a quick list of
things to remember
about your super-secret
spy identity. Fill in the
answers in invisible ink
and carry it around
with you. If you can't
remember your legend,
you can always sneak
away and check this list.

Name (including middle name): _____

Age: _____

Birthday: _____

Year You were Born: _____

Zodiac sign: _____

Address: _____

Phone Number: _____

school: _____

Grade: _____

Teacher: _____

skills: _____

SPOT THE DIFFERENCE

To be a good spy you have to know how to remain undetected. One way of doing that is leaving a room without a trace! Look at the photos below. They are almost exactly the same ... except for ten things.

Can you find the 10 things that are different in each set of photos?

Circle the differences (or write them down on a piece of paper or check the boxes when you find them) and when you think you've found them all, use your UV pen light to see the differences in the bottom photo.

1 _____
2 _____
3 _____
4 _____
5 _____
6 _____
7 _____
8 _____
9 _____
10 _____

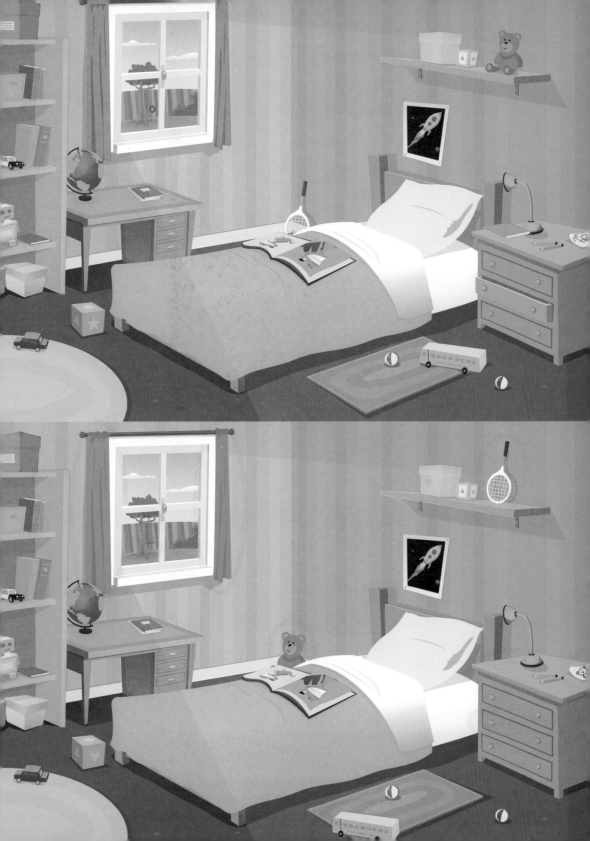

PIGPEN CODE

>ΠΓV ΓV ΊΓꓶOO LꓪO.

Even though pigpen code may look like hieroglyphics or alien speak—or just a big old mess—it's actually a super-secret way to communicate.

In pigpen code, you assign each letter of the alphabet to its own shaped bracket, or "pigpen." When you have a message to communicate, you don't write down the letters. Instead, you draw the brackets that each letter lives in. Just make sure that you and whoever you are communicating with have the key to the code!

Here's a basic example of pigpen code:

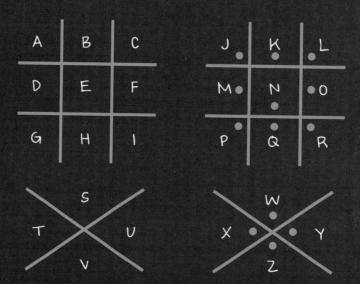

When you write "This message will self-destruct" in pigpen code, it looks like this:

You can use the brackets as written here, or you can create your own pigpen code. Just make sure that each bracket looks different so you don't get any letters mixed up.

⊓: [pigpen coded question]

Q: _____

_____

A: _____

⊓: [pigpen coded question]

Q: _____

_____

A: _____

⊓: [pigpen coded question]

Q: _____

_____

A: _____

Cipher code is one of the most ancient codes known to history. The most famous version of this code, the Caesar Cipher, was used by Julius Caesar, who was kind of a big deal if you lived in Italy 2,000 years ago. It worked so well that it was used by military leaders for hundreds of years.

In this code, one character is substituted for a different character in a specific pattern. The sender and the receiver must both have the correct "key" to understand the message.

One way to create your own cipher code is to write the alphabet in a line, like you see below. Then choose a cipher "key" or number.

Here, we used number 7. So we counted 7 characters and then rewrote the alphabet. Once we ran out of letters, we started the alphabet over again.

A B C D E F G H I J K L M N O P Q R S T U V W X Y Z

1 2 3 4 5 6 7 A B C D E F G H I J K L M N O P Q R S

T U V W X Y Z

Now, you can write out a message, like: "Run. They know everything," and then substitute the bottom, "coded," letters. So your message would look like this:

KNG. MAXR DGHP XOXKRMABGZ.

You can use the cipher code as written here, or you can choose a different code key. Just make sure that whoever you are sending the

USE THE CIPHER CODE ON THE PREVIOUS PAGE TO FIND THE
ANSWERS TO THESE JOKES! USE YOUR UV LIGHT TO REVEAL
THE ANSWERS OR CHECK PAGE 59.

Q: What's the worst thing about trying to throw a party in space?

A: RHN ATOX MH IETGXM!

Q: What kind of music do planets sing?

A: GXIMNGXL!

Q: What is an astronaut's favorite key on a laptop?

A: MAX LITVX URK!

practice cipher code by adding your
own jokes or secret messages here:

SECRETS OF THE UNIVERSE

A grouping of stars that form a shape is called a constellation. Constellations have been named after heroes, animals, objects, or deities, and in many different cultures across the world and throughout history.

Use your UV pen light below to reveal some constellations in the night sky:

WRITE & SHINE!

You can reach for the stars when you design your own sky writing. Draw the straight lines for each letter, then add stars at every corner.

Practice writing the alphabet below in regular pen so you can see how you're doing. Then once you've got the hang of it, use the UV pen to make your writing really shine!

A B C D E F G H I J K L M
N O P Q R S T U V W X Y Z

practice space

write with uv pen

COOL CONSTELLATIONS

Use the UV pen to reveal the shape of each constellation.

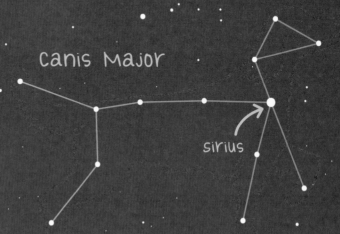

Canis Major

Canis Major contains Sirius, the brightest star in the sky. It represents the hunting dog, Laelaps, from Greek mythology.

Sirius

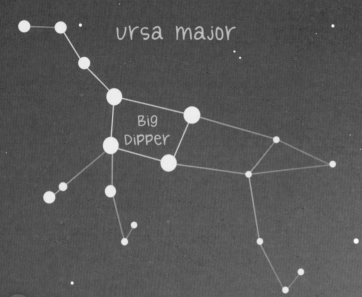

Ursa Major

Big Dipper

The constellation Ursa Major, which is Latin for "the great bear," contains another famous constellation: The Big Dipper!

STAR STORYTELLER

What kinds of shapes would your aliens see in their sky? Draw the shape of constellations you think aliens might see—like a Space-o-Saur or a Giant Sky Narwhal or Some Strange Alien Animal That Hasn't Been Discovered Yet—and use the UV pen to add a star pattern. Then, write the story behind your creation.

This is the
_____
constellation.

_____

_____

_____

_____

_____

_____

PLANET PARTY

We have eight planets in our solar system—and you can see six of them just by looking up at the night sky at the right time. No telescope needed!

IF YOU COULD CREATE A PLANET, WHAT WOULD IT BE LIKE?

Name your planet _____

These three things will DEFINITELY be on my planet: _____
_____

These things will DEFINITELY NOT be on my planet: _____
_____

How many rings does it have? _____

How cold does it get? _____

How hot does it get? _____

How many moons does it have? _____

Now draw your planet! use your imagination—maybe it's a Pizza Planet, or surrounded by ice cream meteors! The sky is the limit!

If there were aliens on your Planet, what would they look like? Draw the aliens who live on your Planet below!

PRANK BREAK!

LOOK!

IMPORTANT

Make sure to keep your pranks light and funny—not mean. And remember... if you play a prank on someone, they just might play a prank on you!

Pranktastic Search-and-Find!

SUPPLIES

- ☐ UV pen
- ☐ Regular pen
- ☐ Paper
- ☐ Bandanna or small box
- ☐ Rubber bands

There's nothing better than a good prank, and this one could keep your target busy for hours!

1 Locate something small that your target uses. It could be a pen, a small toy, the remote control . . . anything, really.

2 Sneak the item away when your target isn't looking. (Don't worry, they'll get it back soon.)

3 Cover it with a bandanna or put it in a small box.

4 Wrap as many rubber bands as you can find around the item in all directions. You can use as few as ten rubber bands (to make it a little annoying) or 50 rubber bands (to make it SUPER annoying).

5 Hide the item.

6 Copy the note and clues on the next page on a piece of paper. Place the note and Clue #1 where your target will be sure to find it. Leave the UV pen next to the note.

7 Hide Clue #2 in a room where you cook food, keep snacks, grab a drink.

8 Hide Clue #3 near a sink.

9 Hide the congratulations note with the rubber band–covered item under your target's pillow.

10 Copy the examples below or create your own!

> Roses are red. Violets are blue.
> How will you find your favorite thing?
> It's up to you!

> clue #1

> clue #2

> clue #3

> Congrats! At last! You've found it! You're grand! Just one more thing left!

DIVE IN!

MYSTERIES OF THE DEEP

In the deep ocean, temperatures are close to freezing and it's almost completely dark, so some creatures can produce their own light. It's called bioluminescence (BY-oh-loo-mi-NEH-sens). You probably already know a creature like this—fireflies!

Use the UV pen light to find the bioluminescent area on these creatures, and then try to draw them on your own. Use your UV pen to highlight their bioluminescent glow.

Draw your own!

Angler Fish

This fish uses its light to lure animals closer so it can eat them with its sharp teeth!

 LOL WHY DID THE ANGLERFISH GO TO THE DOCTOR?
USE YOUR UV PEN TO REVEAL THE ANSWER!

Atolla Jellyfish

Draw your own!

This creature is called the "alarm jelly." When it's threatened, it starts flashing blue lights in a circle—like the light on top of a police car.

HAHA

WHAT MAKES A JELLYFISH LAUGH?

USE YOUR UV PEN TO REVEAL THE ANSWER!

WOULD YOU RATHER...?
DEEP-SEA EDITION

Add your initials next to the option you like best. Then ask a friend to do the same thing. Use the UV pen to see if you and your friend's choices match!

WOULD YOU RATHER...?

Hug a giant octopus   OR   Swim with sharks

Eat sea slime   OR   Drink squid ink

Grow fins   OR   Grow tentacles

Be a big, slow fish   OR   Be a small, fast fish

Have sharp teeth to bite   OR   Camouflage yourself to hide

Have a pet shark   OR   Have a pet octopus

Live in cold water   OR   Live in warm water

Hunt and attack prey   OR   Wait for prey to come to you

Eat all day long   OR   Eat once a day

Color by Number

Use your UV light to reveal the numbers in each section below. Then use the key below to color the picture.

HIDDEN PICTURES

Can you find these 10 objects in the picture?
Reveal the answers by using your UV pen light.

Baseball • Bird
car • cat • Flower
Fork • Lightbulb
Mustache • sunglasses
Top hat & monocle

You're the Captain Now

You are in charge of a submarine expedition to the deepest part of the ocean. You'll be crammed into a small submarine for hours and hours, and you have to depend on your crew to keep you safe. Who will come aboard for the ride?

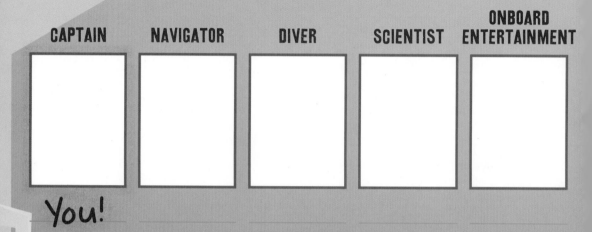

CAPTAIN	NAVIGATOR	DIVER	SCIENTIST	ONBOARD ENTERTAINMENT

You!

To move around your ship, you need a passcode to pass security checkpoints. Write your passcode in UV ink here!

SUPER-SECRET PASSCODE

Once you enter the passcode, you need to scan your thumbprint. Take the UV ink part of your pen and color in your thumb. Make sure to color all over it several times. Then, quickly and firmly, press your thumb onto the scanner to gain entrance!

Design the control panel of your submarine and the view through the windshield. Use the UV pen to help draw the underwater animals that have bioluminescence and any other creepy creatures you may encounter!

SUPER UV-POWER

UV Superpower! Your UV pen gives you the power to see things that no one else can see—kind of like having X-ray vision! Use your superpower on this page. What do you see?

If you could have absolutely any superpower in the world, which one would you pick? And why? Use your super sleuthing skills to find the hidden list of superpowers on this page—or you can dream up your own!

My superpower would be _____

because _____

_____

_____

_____

_____

what do superheroes
like to put in their drinks?
use your uv light to reveal the answer!

IT'S A BIRD! IT'S A PLANE! IT'S... YOU!

Draw a picture of yourself in regular ink, colored pencils, crayons, or whatever you prefer!

When you're finished, draw your super-secret superhero self! Do you have a mask? A cape? A full outfit or any cool gadgets? Include it all!

My superhero name is

_____

Write your super-secret superpowers in UV ink!

_____

_____

_____

SUMMON YOUR SUPER!

As a superhero, you'll need a super signal to call you into action when trouble's brewing. Batman has the Bat-signal. What's yours?

Design your superhero symbol here in invisible ink. Shine your light on it!

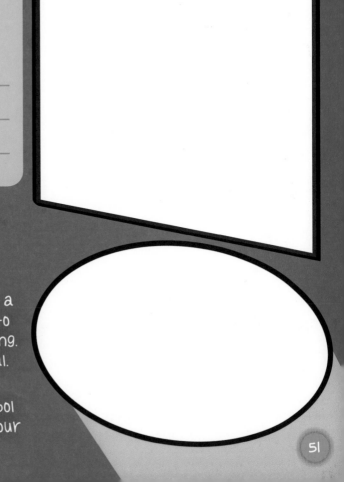

YOUR SUPER SIDEKICK

Every great superhero has a great sidekick. Your super sidekick might be your best friend, your sibling, or even your pet—you just have to make them supercharged!

Draw your super sidekick in the space below just like you drew yourself. Draw your sidekick in regular pen as they look every day and undercover. Then use your UV pen to draw their sidekick look!

My super sidekick is named

_____

My super sidekick superpowers are

_____

BUILD YOUR VILLAIN

Every good superhero is only as good as their super villain!

Now draw your archnemesis in the space below!

My super villain is named
_____

My super villain kryptonite is
_____

CREATE-A-COMIC

What does it look and sound like when you battle your baddie? Practice doodling comic noises here. Use your UV pen to make the noise really POP!

15¢
US

68
PAGES

COMICS
MAGAZINE

SPECIAL EDITION

DIRECT EDITION

00278

23579 02590

THE BEST STORIES
EVERY MONTH

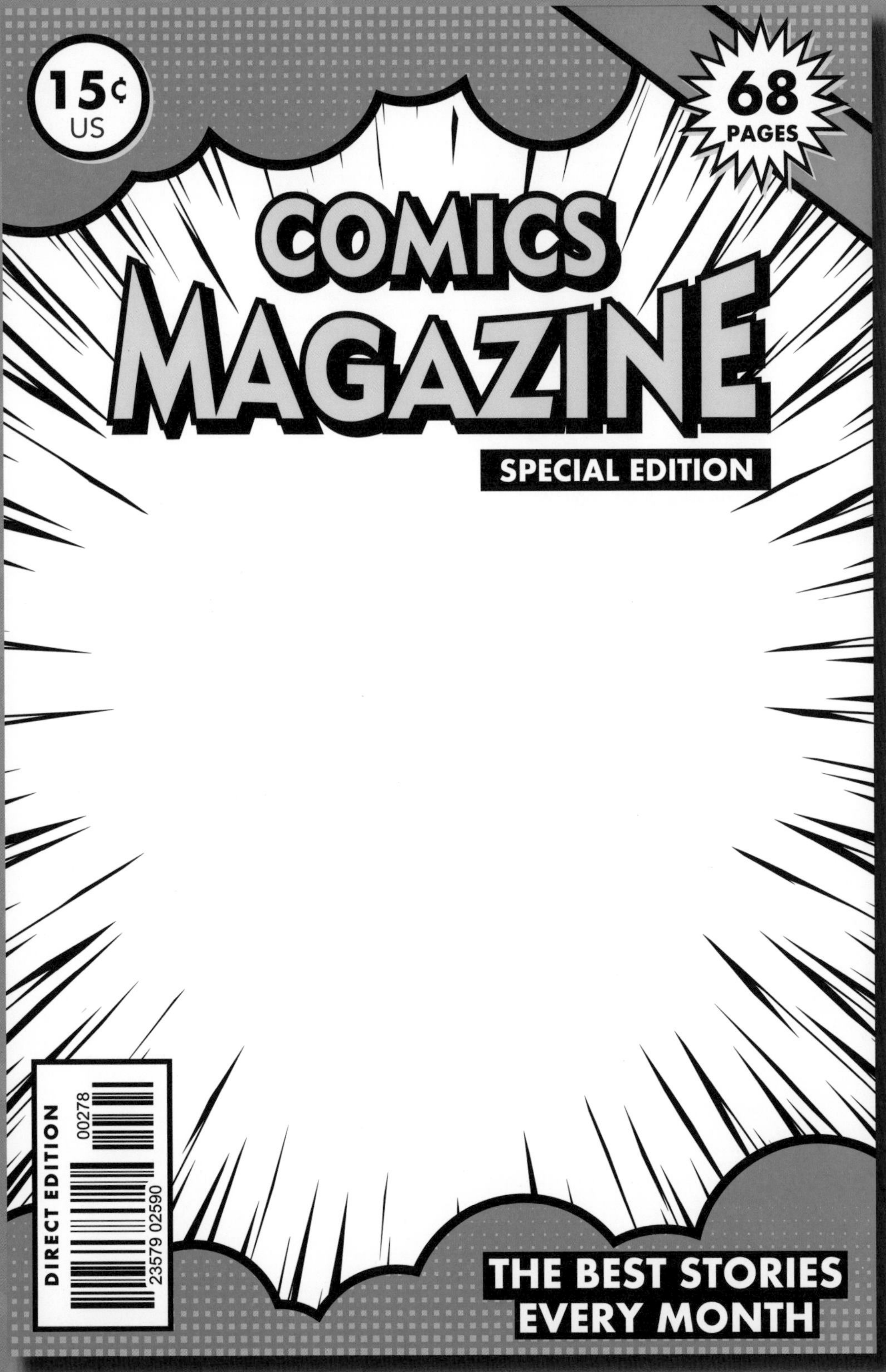

Make your own comic strip using the characters you just created! Use your UV pen to add secret sound FX, thought bubbles, and more!

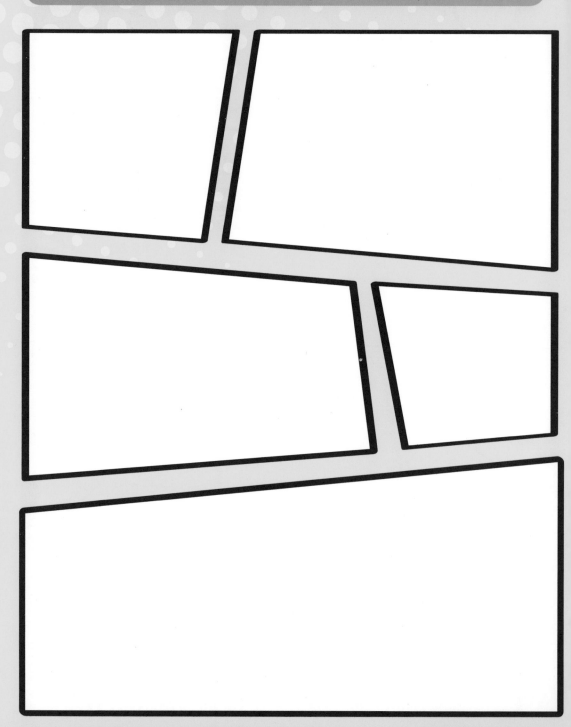

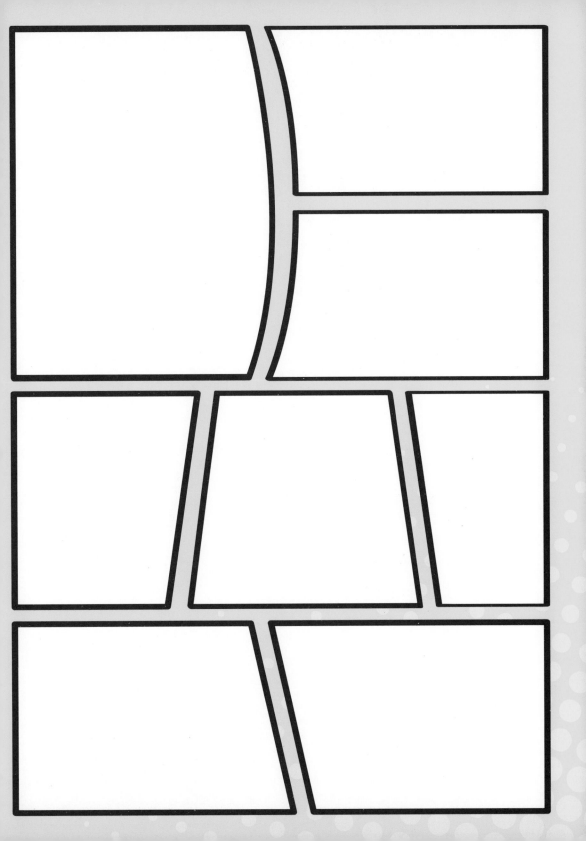

THAT'S NOT ALL, FOLKS!

This book has come to an end, but that doesn't mean the fun has to stop here. Are you *sure* you actually found all the clues and hidden messages, and cracked all the codes in this book? Are you *really* sure? Check your results on the next page. If you weren't quite right, take another crack at it!

Looking for inspiration on what to do next? Revisit pages 9, 11, 13, and 15 for ideas!

Still looking for more? Why not try some of those pranks on pages 22 and 42? Or better yet, invent your own!

Now it's time to go forth and use your UV pen however your heart desires! The *real* fun comes in when you close this book and start to create new games, codes, riddles, and activities all your own. Imagine all the invisible possibilities! What will be the first thing you create? We can't wait to find out.

UH-OH! Has your pen run out of ink? Is the light no longer working? Never fear, flip to page 20 to make your own! If DIY isn't your thing, visit your local Scholastic Book Fair or Shop.Scholastic.com to buy a brand-spankin' new one!

ANSWER KEY

SCAVENGER HUNT CHEAT SHEET (PAGE 10):

Alien Page 41	Backpack Page 14	Crayon Page 20	Dinosaur Page 39
Emoji Page 6	Flashlight Page 21	Guitar Page 30	Hat Page 28
Ice cream Page 18	Jellyfish Page 45	Kite Page 15	Lightning bolt Page 12
Magnifying glass Page 9	Narwhal Page 44	Octopus Page 49	Pig Page 32
Queen Page 38	Rainbow Page 5	Submarine Page 48	Tree Page 14
Uranus Page 40	Volcano Page 30	Wave Page 2	X-ray vision Page 50
	You Page 48	Zap! Page 54	

THERE'S A MYSTERY IN THIS BOOK (PAGE 8):

Clue #1:   Clue #2:   Clue #3:   Clue #4:   Clue #5:   Clue #6:
Page 7   Page 13   Page 20   Page 29   Page 50   Page 60

SO... WHODUNIT? THE CUPCAKE THIEF IS.... **OLLIE!**

THERE'S A RIDDLE IN THIS BOOK (PAGE 12):

Clue #1:   Clue #2:   Clue #3:   Clue #4:
outside   cook   eat   throw

WHAT IS IT? **CORN!**

HIDING IN PLAIN SIGHT (PAGE 14):

1. Whistle   2. Cold   3. Brushes   4. Keyhole
5. Straw   6. Hearts   7. Pom-poms   8. Pocketwatch

DIY INVISIBLE INK JOKE ANSWER (PAGE 20):

They can see straight through them!

DIY INVISIBLE INK JOKE ANSWER (PAGE 21):

They just couldn't see themselves playing on it!

SPOT THE DIFFERENCE (PAGE 30):

1. Bear on shelf replaced with tennis racket
2. Book is missing from nightstand
3. School bus moved on the floor
4. Tennis racket in corner replaced with bear
5. Star on cube replaced with heart
6. Ball (next to robot) changed from red to green
7. Tire swing replaced with regular swing
8. Curtains changed to green
9. Pink book on shelf changed to blue book
10. Drawer on nightstand is now closed

PIGPEN CODE JOKE ANSWERS (PAGE 33):

Q: Why was the tarantula wearing a disguise?
A: Because it was a spyder!

Q: What is a spy's favorite kind of shoes?
A: Sneakers!

Q: What do you call an alligator in a vest?
A: An investigator

CIPHER CODE JOKE ANSWERS (PAGE 35):

· You have to planet!   · Neptunes!   · The space bar!

DIVE IN JOKE ANSWER (PAGE 44):

He was feeling light-headed!

DIVE IN JOKE ANSWER (PAGE 45):

Ten tickles!

CREDITS

Manufacturing & Development: Wing Seto
Designer: Vanessa Han
Illustrator: Jeanine Murch
Writer: Rosie Colosi
Editor: Valerie Wire
Product Development Manager: Gina Kim
Product Integrity: Karen Fuchs
Special Thanks: Stacy Lellos, Teresa Imperato, Netta Rabin, Caitlin Harpin, Cormac McEvoy, and Hannah Rogge

Get creative with more from KLUTZ

Looking for more goof-proof activities, sneak peeks, and giveaways?
Find us online!

KlutzCertified   KlutzCertified   KlutzCertified   KlutzCertified   Klutz

Klutz.com • thefolks@klutz.com • 1-800-737-4123